"How-to" Guide

Personal
Spiritual
Development
Analysis

Evening Star Enterprise

Wilmore, KY 40390

Rick Gray

Evening Star Enterprise, Inc.
PO Box 254
Wilmore, KY 40390

World Wide Web: www.eveningstarenterprise.com

E-mail: Rgray@eveningstarenterprise.com

© 2008 by Rick Gray

All rights reserved. No part of this book may be reproduced, distributed or transmitted in any form without the prior written permission from Evening Star Enterprise, except in the case of brief quotations embodied in critical reviews and other non-commercial uses permitted by copyright law.

ISBN: 978-0-9790210-3-9
ISBN: 0-9790210-3-0

Printed in the United States of America

Dedication

The PSDA is adapted from the work of Dr. J. Robert Clinton and is dedicated to his years of service and ministry.

Thank you, Dr. Clinton for your contribution to the study of Christian Leadership.

<u>*The Making of a Leader*</u>

Reading his book first will help make this guide easier to complete.

The Personal Spiritual Development Analysis

Introduction   page 7

PART ONE: The Title Page   page 9

> *Develop a heading that identifies this study as a spiritual autobiography. Consider a statement like:*
>
> *"An intimate look into the spiritual journey of . . ." or simply "Personal Spiritual Development Analysis"*

PART TWO: Expanded Personal Biography   page 11

> *Is comprised of demographic information about yourself that will help locate your age, gifts, etc.*

PART THREE: The Personal Timeline   page 13

> *This is a continuum that begins with the date of your birth and flows to the present time. It is a structured picture of the major transition points, secondary transition points, and formative encounters of your life.*

PART FOUR: The Snapshot   page 21

> *This is a single spaced 3 to 5 page narrative that provides a picture of your journey to-date.*

PART FIVE: The Formative Encounters   page 27

>   *Formative Encounters are those people, activities, events and/or anything else that God uses in the spiritual development of a person.*

PART SIX: The Discovery Statement   page 33

>   *This statement should be a one-page indication of your significant learning from doing this project.*

PART SEVEN: Appendix ("Sample Study")   page 35

About the Authors   page 87

The Personal Spiritual Development Analysis

Introduction

The Personal Spiritual Development Analysis is designed to help you know that God has been at work within you, molding and shaping you spiritually, from a time long before you embraced him. This exercise will help you to see that he actually began the work of forming you even before you knew that he cared for and loved you.

Your personal spiritual development analysis is a personal spiritual timeline of your life from early childhood to today. However, rather than trying to write a spiritual autobiography of your entire life, limit your reflections to those events which have had special significance to your faith walk and spiritual formation. You are to identify key events in your life, recast these events as "formative encounters," and apply a spiritual significance to the event as a lesson learned (see the example provided). By breaking the events of your life down into formative encounters (single significant events) and giving a spiritual significance to that event, you will begin to see how God is using the events in your life to shape you. This understanding should help you understand that there are deep reasons for the events of our lives.

As you develop your **PSDA**, you will find yourself reliving memories of events that have been very formational in your personal development. Permit yourself to pray, laugh, cry and even heal where necessary as the Holy Spirit guides you back across your life's experiences. Some memories no doubt will be painful and some may cause feelings of shame or regret. Don't dwell on the negatives but rather permit the Holy Spirit to help you look beyond them to see how God has always been standing at your side guiding you to this very moment. Take comfort in this knowledge and be assured that "God has begun a good work in you and will perform it until the day of Jesus Christ." (Phil. 1:6).

1

The Title Page

Begin your PSDA by completing a title page. Consider including pictures to make the page more interesting and personal. The next page will give you an idea of what your title page should look like. Remember to be creative. Your title page does not have to look exactly like the sample.

*The Personal
Spiritual Development
Analysis*

of

[Your Name]

Date:

2

Expanded Personal Biography

Your personal biography will provide demographic information to anyone who may read your study at a later date. It will also help you remember when your spiritual autobiography was first undertaken as you add to it in later years.

You do not have to limit yourself to the demographic headings that have been suggested. Include any additional heading and information that you think will be helpful knowledge for someone reading this study at a later date.

Expanded Personal Biography

Date information compiled for this study:

Name:

Current Age:

You do not have to limit yourself to these headings. They represent the minimal information in your finished study.

Personal Time-Line Dates:

Date this study was completed:

Age when I embraced Jesus Christ as Savior:

Age when I discovered my Spiritual Gift(s)

Spiritual Gifts mix:

    Primary gift   ———————————
    Secondary gift   ———————————
    Secondary gift   ———————————
    Secondary gift   ———————————

Talents:

    Primary talent   ———————————
    Secondary talent ———————————

Major roles I've occupied:

3

The Personal Timeline

Your personal timeline should be constructed as a continuum drawn along a horizontal line and not as a vertical dyad. Pay close attention to the example provided.

Constructing a Personal Timeline.

Note: This is how a continuum looks.

Major Developmental Era	Major Developmental Era	Major Developmental Era

1967 — 1996 — 2005 — 2008

Beginnings ◄─────────────────► Present

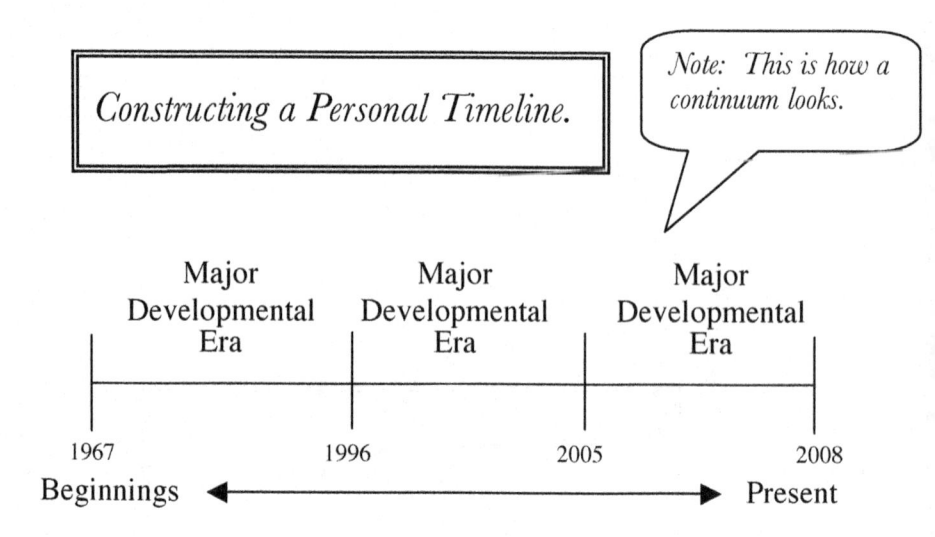

Your time line should have a beginning date. Have it begin with your birth and establish a new date for each Major Developmental Era. Once you have your Major Transition Points identified and located on the time line, you will need to give each a heading. For example your earliest Formative Encounter might have occurred while you were a child growing up in your parents' home. You would understand this to be a part of your early formational period. Locate this period and give it a heading to reflect its significance. In our example below, *Foundational Base* represents the first developmental paradigm or early formational period. *Ministry Validation Through Preparation* represents the second paradigm and *Growing Influence* represents the third paradigm.

In *The Making of a Leader*, Clinton identifies six major phases. They serve as a helpful guide. We took Clinton's six phases and collapsed them down to three major paradigms to more accurately reflect the development of this writer. You should do the same.

Next, locate the secondary transition points in your life. A transition point is a significant happening that caused a changing of the direction your life was going. Examples of transition points include: conversion experience, going off to college, relocation, getting married, etc. We all have those pivotal points in our experiences. Once you have identified your personal transition points, give them a title unique to your life.

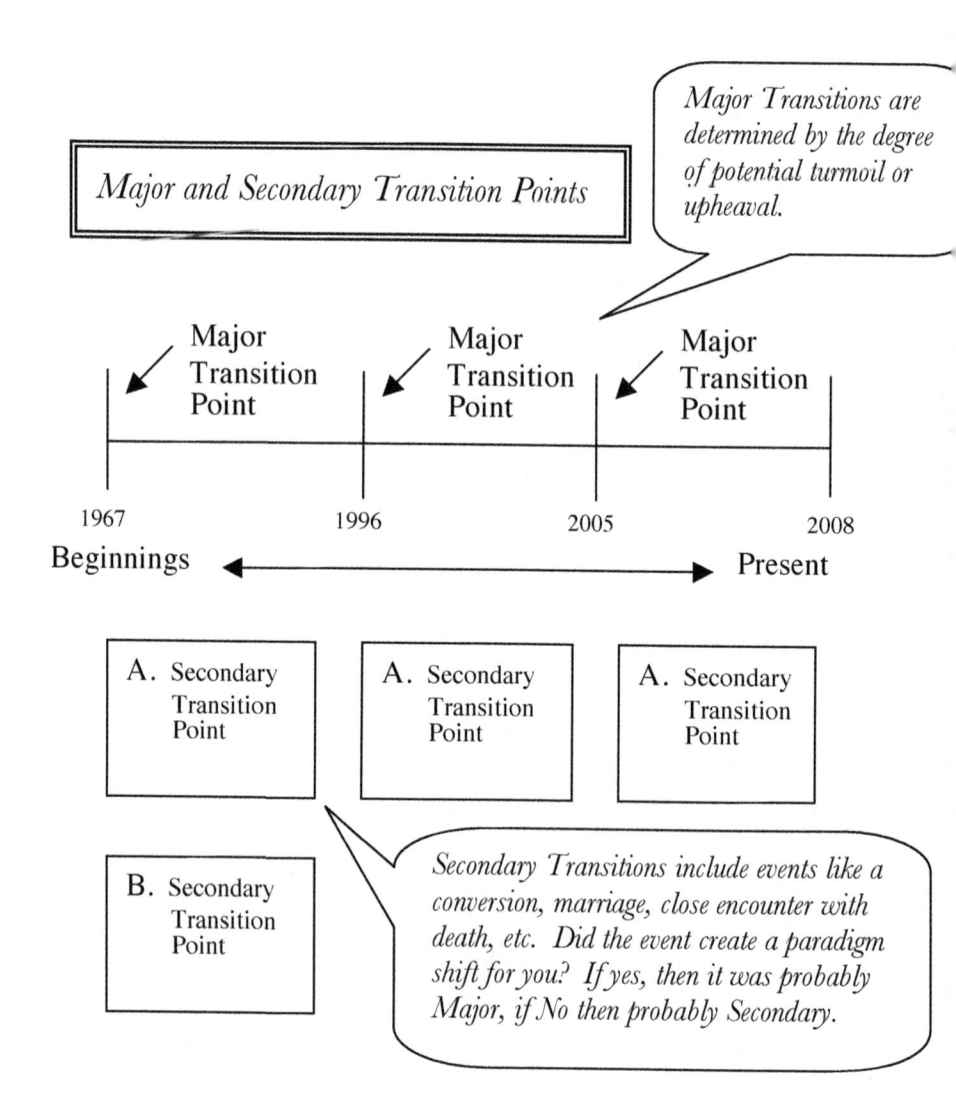

Major and Secondary Transition Points

Major Transitions are determined by the degree of potential turmoil or upheaval.

- Major Transition Point
- Major Transition Point
- Major Transition Point

1967 — 1996 — 2005 — 2008

Beginnings ⟵⟶ Present

- A. Secondary Transition Point
- A. Secondary Transition Point
- A. Secondary Transition Point

- B. Secondary Transition Point

Secondary Transitions include events like a conversion, marriage, close encounter with death, etc. Did the event create a paradigm shift for you? If yes, then it was probably Major, if No then probably Secondary.

Note that the Foundational Base paradigm has two sections. Section A contains all of those formation encounters that were important for helping this individual through infancy and early adolescence. The event which separated section A from section B was a conversion experience and section B contains all of those formation encounters which helped shape this person's early Christian walk. Combined, these transition headings, along with the titles you give your major developmental eras will form the titles for the SnapShot .

The PSDA

Major Developmental and Secondary Transition Headings

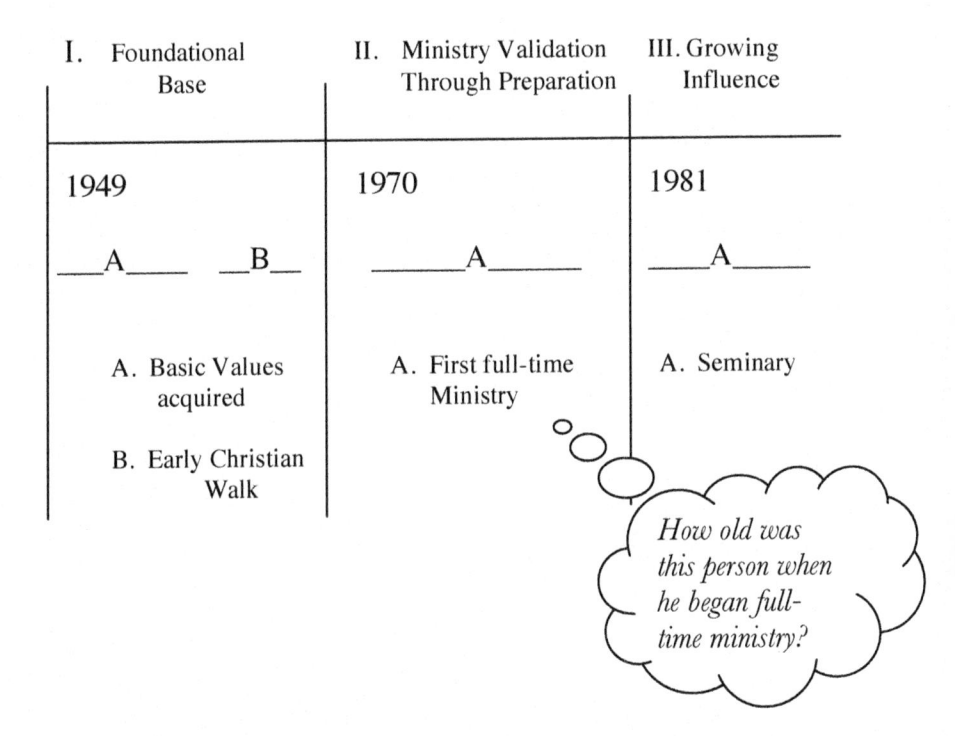

I. Foundational Base | II. Ministry Validation Through Preparation | III. Growing Influence

1949 | 1970 | 1981

__A____ __B__ | _____A_____ | ___A___

A. Basic Values acquired

B. Early Christian Walk

A. First full-time Ministry

A. Seminary

How old was this person when he began full-time ministry?

Note: You can tell the age of the individual when the transitions occurred. Also, note how the headings of the various transitions have been personalized to this particular individual. You can also tell that this person was 32 years old when he entered seminary. The last formative encounter under the Ministry Validation Through Preparation section of this study should help us to understand why the paradigm shift occurred.

Inserting your Age into the Timeline

Once you have determined your major developmental paradigms, identified the dates where the paradigms began and sectioned each era, you are ready to insert your age into the time line. You should note your age at the beginning of each new developmental paradigm and the location where the majority of the formation encounters occurred.

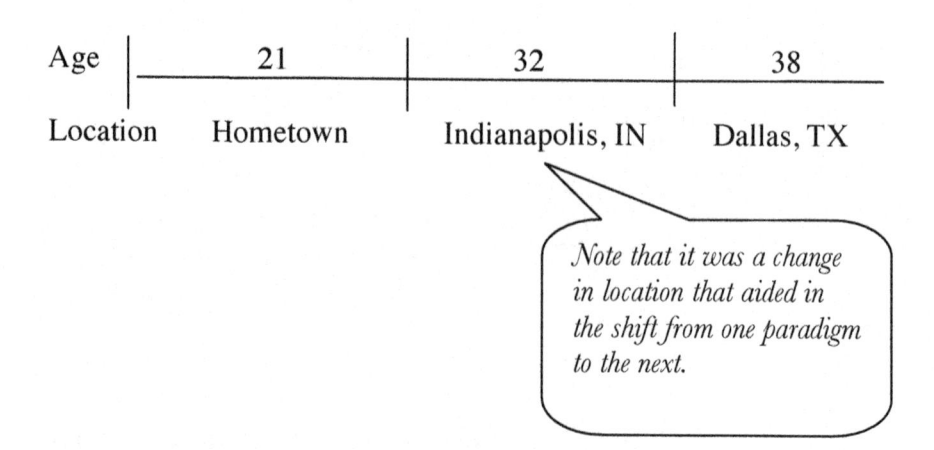

Age	21	32	38
Location	Hometown	Indianapolis, IN	Dallas, TX

Note that it was a change in location that aided in the shift from one paradigm to the next.

Listing Formative Encounters

Next on your PSDA is the actual inclusion of your headings for your *Formative Encounters*.

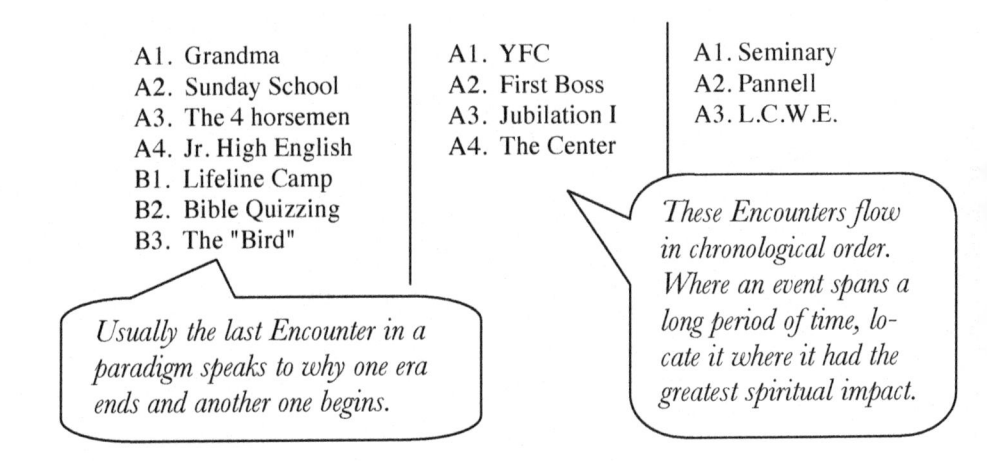

A1. Grandma
A2. Sunday School
A3. The 4 horsemen
A4. Jr. High English
B1. Lifeline Camp
B2. Bible Quizzing
B3. The "Bird"

A1. YFC
A2. First Boss
A3. Jubilation I
A4. The Center

A1. Seminary
A2. Pannell
A3. L.C.W.E.

Usually the last Encounter in a paradigm speaks to why one era ends and another one begins.

These Encounters flow in chronological order. Where an event spans a long period of time, locate it where it had the greatest spiritual impact.

Note the lettering and numbering of the Formative Encounters and how they relate to the Transition Points on the Timeline. There is no limit on the number of Formative Encounters that you can identify but you probably won't want to have less than 30. The Formative Encounters are centered around the context, events and people who have been significant in your spiritual journey thus far. You should write out the story of the event in one page or less. Remember to leave space at the bottom of the page to make a spiritual application for the lesson (how did this event help shape you spiritually? Is there a universal spiritual principle?) Formative Encounters flow in chronological order thru your life. Developmental Paradigms tend to overlap so be creative in labeling them. Make the titles reflective of your life's journey.

A Complete Personalized Timeline

I. Foundational Base	II. Ministry Validation Through Preparation	III. Growing Influence
1949 __A__ __B__ A. Basic Values Acquired B. Early Christian Walk	**1970** _____A_____ A. First full-time Ministry	**1981** _____A_____ A. Seminary
21 →	32 →	38 →
Hometown A1. Grandma A2. Sunday School A3. The 4 horsemen A4. Jr. High English B1. Lifeline Camp B2. Bible Quizzing B3. The "Bird"	**Indianapolis, IN** A1. YFC A2. First Boss A3. Jubilation I A4. The Center	**Dallas, TX** A1. Seminary A2. Pannell A3. L.C.W.E.

4

If reading this was all that a person was able to do, it should still give them a good picture of who you are.

The SnapShot

This is a single spaced 3 to 5 page narrative that provides a picture of your journey to-date.

By reading the SnapShot, one should gain an overview of the significant occurrences in your life. This overview should flow through your life chronologically.

We've included an entire SnapShot so that you can get a feel for the length and quality of the reflection.

> *Here is an example of a SnapShot. Though this example is written in 3rd person, you should write in 1st person. Note how the title for each section exactly matches the Major Developmental and Secondary Transition titles in the Timeline.*

I. FOUNDATIONAL BASE

A. Basic Values

Most of Amanda's earliest exposures to the Lord were through the religious nature of her mother, father, and grandmother. They continually prayed together and her father read the Bible to them on Sundays. Her parents were a great source of Godliness for their children by modeling holiness and Christian charity. Although they were slaves, Amanda's parents harbored an attitude of gracious abandonment and gratitude toward God.

Early on in her life, Amanda encountered the power of prayer, which led to her family's freedom. Amanda's mother and grandmother continually prayed for the deliverance of their Mistress, Miss Celie, and eventually Miss Celie was saved. Miss Celie became a committed Christian and prayed with Amanda's family constantly. Miss Celie became very ill and when she was approaching death, she granted Amanda and her family freedom.

At age 13, Amanda attended a revival at a Methodist camp and was touched by the Holy Spirit. She did not accept Christ, however this experience opened her eyes further to the reality of God. Amanda struggled because she was forced to sit in the back of the church and could not receive teaching at Sunday school until the white children were finished. This led to Amanda's search for a greater understanding of Jesus Christ.

B. Early Christian Walk

A lack of discipline and exposure to an atheistic book soon led Amanda to doubt the existence of God, which was a very isolating experience for her because she was ashamed to tell anyone. At this point Amanda was living with a white family she worked for and did not have contact with her family. Her aunt visited her one day and Amanda asked her aunt how she could possibly believe in God. Her aunt scolded her and assured her that she was "raised better than that."

Amanda grew up rather fast and got married before she was ready. Marriage proved to be no source of peace for Amanda so she began searching for answers again.

Her husband was an alcoholic and did not want Amanda pursuing her faith. Shortly after her wedding, Amanda became violently ill and nearly died. While experiencing a deadly fever and numerous blackouts, Amanda had a vision in which she was preaching the Word of God before hundreds of people. This led Amanda to begin searching for the Lord again.

After the vision, Amanda began attending various revivals, but never felt she needed to pray at the altar to be converted. She wanted to wait for the perfect moment to be converted—her timing rather than God's. One night at a tent meeting she felt terribly convicted and realized how full of pride she had become. This feeling of guilt led Amanda to feel worthless and unworthy of God's love and she began praying to the stars and moon to tell Jesus she was sorry. At this point Amanda began seeking salvation.

II. MINISTRY VALIDATION THROUGH PREPARATION

A. First Full-time Ministry

The Lord began to use Amanda for various kinds of evangelism. Amanda consistently distributed Tracts to various people she encountered. On a number of occasions she failed to hand out Tracts to people that she felt God was leading her to give them to. She quickly overcame her fears, however, by giving a Tract to a white man, who received his salvation due to her obedience to the Lord. Amanda had very little money, but she always managed to buy Tracts.

Amanda became actively involved at the Green Street Church and began attending various Camp Meetings and holiness revivals. It was at one of these meetings that Amanda shared her testimony and the people seemed to be greatly moved by the Spirit. Amanda also began a prayer meeting for those who wanted to grow closer to the Lord.

At one of the Holiness Camp Meetings, Amanda asked the Lord what he would have from her, and she received the message, "GO." Amanda did not understand what this meant at first, but she soon came to realize that the Lord was calling her to preach the word.

III. GROWING INFLUENCE

A. Seminary

Okay. You got us. The narrative of this SnapShot was not written to correlate with these titles but yours should.

As soon as Amanda received her message from the Lord to "go," the Lord began providing opportunities for her to minister. She continued to attend revival meetings, but began to speak and sing at the meetings on a regular basis. The Lord seemed to move in mighty ways whenever she preached and prayed, and her fellow Christian friends recognized her anointing.

Early on in her ministry, Amanda became interested in mission work. She attended a camp meeting where a missionary spoke about missions in India and South America. Amanda immediately felt a tug on her heart to be involved in missions, but wondered why there were not more missionaries in Africa. Her pursuit of missions in Africa would eventually lead to her participation in African missions.

Amanda faced a great deal of opposition despite her ministry success. Wherever Amanda went to speak, there were whites who opposed her because she was black and she was a woman. Amanda soon came to grips with who she was in Christ's eyes and confronted racism and sexism head on. God used Amanda to free many people of racism as well as sexism.

Word of Amanda's anointing and powerful speaking soon got around. A group of women from England attended one of her meetings and insisted that she come and speak at a worldwide conference in England. After a great deal of prayer, Amanda accepted and went to England. Amanda found a great deal of acceptance in England and was amazed by the lack of racism and oppression. She spoke many times throughout England and gained the respect of the English people.

Amanda finally got the opportunity to participate in missions when an English Missionary invited her to India. Amanda accepted and eventually spent several years in India. Amanda faced sickness, disease, poverty and danger the entire time she was in India, but never gave up. While many of her missionary partners grew weary and faint of heart, Amanda continued to evangelize the people of India with all her might. Countless numbers of Indians were converted because of Amanda's faithfulness.

Likewise, Amanda participated in missions in Africa. While in Africa, Amanda developed a sense of pride in her heritage and her people. Amanda developed a "Paul-like" ministry in Africa and traveled back and forth between several churches, ministering to and growing the people. Amanda also adopted a native girl who had been sold to an abusive man. Her experiences in Africa developed her leadership skills even further, making her one of the most versatile and effective missionaries of her day.

Even in her old age, Amanda continued her ministry. She became very active in social justice movements and provided a source of inspiration to African Americans throughout the nation. Her final endeavor was the opening of an orphanage where children could be cared for and receive an education.

5

This is one shaping event that may or may not span a large number of years.

The Formative Encounter

Focus in on the lesson and how the learning has affected you.

The development of your Formative Encounters is probably the most important aspect of your PSDA. It is through this portion of the study that you will see that God has never been absent from your journey.

There are four sections to the Formative Encounter. They are:

> The Demographic Section
> The Encounter
> The Interpretation
> The Spiritual Principle

| SECTION ONE: The Demographic Section |

Can you tell which Formative Encounter should come next? Check the Timeline!!

Development Paradigm: **FOUNDATIONAL BASE**

Pride in Faithfulness
(Grandma)

Formative Encounter Type: Personal Discovery

Time: Age 11

We made up this "Type" but Clinton offers a large variety of types in his book.

Note the four sections that comprise the demographics of your formative encounter. They are:

(1) The Developmental Paradigm in which the encounter occurred (foundational base above).

(2) The Title of the encounter. This title should exactly match the title found in your Personal Timeline.

(3) The Type of encounter (personal discovery above)

(4) The Time or approximate age when the encounter took place. *Remember the encounters should flow chronologically.*

| SECTION TWO: The Story of the Encounter |

Stories flow from your own life's experiences!!

The Encounter:

Grandma taught me many things that I can only now appreciate. Many of the things she taught me were accomplished by her negative example rather than deliberate molding, even so, she did instill in me a pride in faithfulness and I am sure that she realized that she had done so.

My grandmother was a Godly woman. Often during the years I lived with her, I would see her pouring herself into the Word. She never shared with me about spiritual things, never told me what she was reading, never bought me a Bible, but she did make sure that I was in Sunday School and Church every Sunday. Also, she taught me to say a simple prayer each night before I went to bed.

"Now I lay me down to sleep, I pray the Lord my soul to keep. If I should die before I wake, I pray the Lord my soul to take."

It was all the prayer I knew and I recited it every night before going to bed. One Sunday morning in Sunday school, the teacher asked for a show of hands for everyone who prayed every day. I was the only one to raise my hand. The teacher just ignored me as though she didn't really believe me, but that was all right with me.

SECTION THREE: What the Encounter means to you

How did the Encounter impact who you are today?

Interpretative Comment:

Even at that young age, I knew for myself that I was sincere and received a sense of personal satisfaction in knowing that I had been faithful. It didn't matter to me that I wasn't believed.

How has this encounter shaped how you are today in terms of the "beingness" of who you are.

SECTION FOUR: A Universal principle

You should be able to identify a spiritual principle that applies to everyone.

Spiritual Application or Principle:

Bring up a child in the way that he should go and when he is old he will not depart from it.

What is the universal principle or truth that flows from the Encounter?

Here is an example of a completed Formative Encounter

Development Paradigm:　　FOUNDATIONAL BASE
Pride in Faithfulness **(Grandma)**
Formative Encounter Type: Personal Discovery
Time: Age 11

The Encounter:

Grandma taught me many things that I can only now appreciate. Many of the things she taught me were accomplished by her negative example rather than deliberate molding, even so, she did instill in me a pride in faithfulness and I am sure that she realized that she had done so.

My grandmother was a Godly woman. Often during the years I lived with her, I would see her pouring herself into the Word. She never shared with me about spiritual things, never told me what she was reading, never bought me a Bible, but she did make sure that I was in Sunday School and Church every Sunday. Also, she taught me to say a simple prayer each night before I went to bed.

> *"Now I lay me down to sleep, I pray the Lord my soul to keep.*
> *If I should die before I wake, I pray the Lord my soul to take."*

It was all the prayer I knew and I recited it every night before going to bed. One Sunday morning in Sunday school, the teacher asked for a show of hands for everyone who prayed every day. I was the only one to raise my hand. The teacher just ignored me as though she didn't really believe me, but that was all right with me.

Interpretative Comment:

Even at that young age, I knew for myself that I was sincere and received a sense of personal satisfaction in knowing that I had been faithful. It didn't matter to me that I wasn't believed.

Spiritual Application or Principle:

Bring up a child in the way that he should go and when he is old, he will not depart from it.

6

The Discovery Statement

Once you have completed your Timeline, SnapShot and Formative Encounters, end the study with a two or three paragraph reflection which focuses on what you have learned about how God has been using the events of your life to mold and shape you into the spiritual being you are becoming, this is *The Discovery Statement*. Also include how the execution of this project affected you at this point in your development.

> *The following is an example of a Discovery Statement.*

As I write this final observation, I am exhausted. I found writing my own personal spiritual development analysis to be one of the most difficult projects of my experience. Part of the difficulty lie in the fact that the study is so personal. I also regret not having had the time to contribute two or three Formative Encounters every week so that I would not have had to do 90% of the work over the last week.

This study has helped me to look into my past. Sometimes it wasn't easy to write about the hard things in my life. But other times when I could see where God was in certain events, people and places, it helped increase my faith.

I hope to expand this study in the future. I love writing and reflecting on what God has done in my life and I am excited to see what he has in store for me. I know that with God, it will be worth it.

The Appendix

Dwight L. Moody

> Actually because it was written by someone other than Moody it is a LDS (Leadership Development Study) but we asked John to do it as a PSDA. We are grateful for his permission to use his study here.

PERSONAL SPIRITUAL DEVELOPMENT ANALYSIS

of

Dwight L. Moody

by
John Banter

Leadership Development Study
Dwight L. Moody

Table of Contents

INTRODUCTION	40
PERSONAL TIMELINE	41
SNAPSHOT	43
Paradigm I – Foundations	43
Basic Values Acquired	43
Early Christian Walk	44
Paradigm II – Inner-Life Growth	44
Full-Time Ministry	44
Paradigm III – Practical Theology	45
YMCA	45
Paradigm IV – Ministry Maturing	45
Home Front Ministry	45
Abroad Ministry	46
Paradigm V – Developing Education	47
First Schools	47
Bible Institute	47
Paradigm VI – Finishing Well	48
Innovations	48
FORMATIVE ENCOUNTERS	49
Developmental Era I – *Foundations*	49
Foundations Phase: Death of Father	49
Foundations Phase: Religious Interest	50
Foundations Phase: Isaiah's Desertion	51
Foundations Phase: Compassionate Teacher	52
Foundations Phase: Good Samaritan	53
Foundations Phase: Conversion	54
Developmental Era II – *Inner-Life Growth*	55
Inner-Life Growth Phase: Mentors	55
Inner-Life Growth Phase: Sunday School Ministry	56
Inner-Life Growth Phase: Valuable Workers	57
Inner-Life Growth Phase: Soul Struggle	58

Developmental Era III – Practical Theology ... 59
   Practical Theology Phase: YMCA ... 59
   Practical Theology Phase: Marriage ... 60
   Practical Theology Phase: 72nd Illinois Volunteers ... 61
   Practical Theology Phase: Changing Ministry ... 63
   Practical Theology Phase: Ministry Controversy ... 64
   Practical Theology Phase: O. O. Howard ... 65

Developmental Era IV – Ministry Maturing ... 67
   Ministry Maturing Phase: Illinois Street Church ... 67
   Ministry Maturing Phase: Presidency ... 68
   Ministry Maturing Phase: Personal Trouble ... 70
   Ministry Maturing Phase: England ... 72
   Ministry Maturing Phase: Henry Moorhouse ... 73
   Ministry Maturing Phase: YMCA Fire ... 74
   Ministry Maturing Phase: Trail by Fire ... 75
   Ministry Maturing Phase: Britain Revival ... 76
   Ministry Maturing Phase: Developing Leaders ... 77

Developmental Era V – Developing Education ... 78
   Developing Education Phase: New Strategy ... 78
   Developing Education Phase: Northfield Seminary ... 79
   Developing Education Phase: Mount Hermon ... 80
   Developing Education Phase: Chicago Bible Institute ... 81

Developmental Era VI – Finishing Well ... 82
   Finishing Well Phase: Publishing ... 82
   Finishing Well Phase: Christian Conferences ... 84

Discovery Statement ... 85

Bibliography ... 86

About the Authors ... 87

Introduction

I have read some of Dwight L. Moody's work before I began this endeavor to do a Leadership Development Study of his life. I know that he was an interesting character and had wonderful ministries. From all of this I feel I could learn from him, both in his mistakes and his successes. Upon completion of this leadership study, I hope that I can look back and see:

1. How his life impacted others that he came into contact with, both in ministry and in his everyday life.

2. How his spiritual life impacted his ministry.

3. How his leadership affected his ministry.

The study takes the reader through Dwight L. Moody's entire life to see each significant event that led to a change in Dwight Moody's life. The study begins with the death of his father and ends toward the end of his life when he begins the different Christian conferences. Each phase of his life, following Clinton's basic examples, was marked by process items contributing to the spiritual development of the leader.

Personal Timeline

I. Foundations		II. Inner-Life Growth	III. Practical Theology	
1837	1854	1856	1861	1861
A	B	A	A	B
A. Basic Values Acquired B. Early Christian Walk		A. First full-time Ministry	A. YMCA B. Civil War	
17		23	28	
A. Northfield, MA B. Boston, MA		A. Chicago	A/B. Chicago	
Aa. Death of Father Ab. Religious Interest Ac. Isaiah's Desertion Ad. Compassionate Teacher Ae. Good Samaritan Ba. Conversion		Aa. Mentors Ab. Sunday School Ministry Ac. Valuable Workers Ad. Soul Struggle	Aa. YMCA Ab. Marriage Ba. 72nd Illinois Bb. Changing Ministry Bc. Ministry Controversy Bd. O.O. Howard	

IV Ministry Maturing	V. Developing Education	VI Finishing Well
1865 1877 A / B	1877 1889 A | B	1895 A/B
A. Home Front Ministry B. Abroad Ministry	A. First Schools B. Bible Institute	A/B. Innovations
47	52	58
A. Chicago B. England	A. Northfield B. Chicago	A. Chicago B. Northfield
Aa. Ill St. Church Ab. Presidency Ac. Personal Troubles Ba. England Bb. Henry Moorhouse Ad. YMCA Fire Ae. Trial by Fire Bc. Britain Revival Bd. Developing Leaders	Aa. New Strategy Aa. Northfield Seminary Ac. Mount Hermon Ba. Chicago Bible Institute	Aa. Publishing Ba. Conferences

Snapshot

Phase I – Foundations

Basic Skills Acquired

Dwight Moody's early childhood was marked by the death of his father, Edwin Moody. Moody's father's death left the family in debt and throughout his childhood the family lived in poverty. His mother, Betsy, struggled to keep the family together even though the odds were against her and many people advised her to split the family up. Betsy refused to let the family be split apart and worked hard to pay off the debt and still raise the family in their single parent home.

Soon after Edwin Moody's death, Dwight's mother seemed to gain an interest in religion. To the rescue came Reverend Oliver Everett, who was the pastor of the Northfield Presbyterian Church. Everett helped bring Betsy Moody into the faith and more importantly her children. Not only did he provide the support of the church community, he offered material assistance to help Betsy keep the family together. His example of Christ to the Moody family was exactly what they needed after the death of Edwin Moody.

In 1843, Isaiah Moody, the oldest boy who would have taken up the father role in the Moody household disappeared mysteriously. His desertion of the family broke Betsy Moody's spirit for a time and she seemed to age quickly after that. Also, without giving a hint or saying good-bye, it was thought that Isaiah had died until he randomly reappeared in Northfield nearly thirteen years later.

Dwight Moody's childhood was also marked by two people's incredible Godliness. This first was a new schoolteacher who came to teach at the school that the Moody children randomly attended. She came in and changed the way things were done for example by starting off school each day with prayer. She also refused to enforce discipline with a whip but rather by loving the children. Dwight came face to face with this love when he was disobedient once and he saw first hand the compassion the schoolteacher had for the children.

The second individual to impact Moody was an old man who shared the whole Gospel story with young Dwight when he was very homesick working in the town of Greenfield doing chores. When the old man saw that Dwight was a new boy in Greenfield, he stopped him on the street and told him of God's love for him and how he sent his only Son to die for his sins. Then he gave Dwight a bright new cent and went about his way. To young Moody, the old man seemed to be God himself.

Early Christian Walk

Upon entering the city of Boston, Dwight was homeless and jobless. He found himself sleeping on benches and not eating meals. He got a job as a sales clerk in his uncle's shoe store on the condition that he attend both Sunday school and church. In the Sunday school class at the Mount Vernon Congregational Church, Dwight met Edward Kimball. Dwight came to greatly respect Kimball and when the Lord led Kimball to speak with him one day Kimball did so, leading young Dwight to Christ.

Phase II – Inner-Life Growth

First Full Time Ministry

When Dwight moved to Chicago, his interest in earning wealth and his zealous new spirituality were in conflict. He began to speak up at church meetings and his speaking led to a woman, "Mother" Phillips to offer him free room and board if he would give up the shoe trade and go into full-time ministry. He thought the idea was ridiculous, but "Mother" Phillips did teach him the importance of prayer, Bible study, scripture memorization, and disciple making. During the same time, Dwight also met J. B. Stillson who became his mentor showing him how to study the Bible in a careful and systematic fashion.

He then found himself being involved more and more in children's ministry. His heart was warmed for those in poverty in an area of Chicago called "the Sands." Dwight rented out an old saloon and began a Sunday school ministry for the children of that area. The services soon became very popular and it was a thriving ministry. Each session included singing, prayer, Bible readings, stories, and at the same time, fights, screaming, and laughter.

In this ministry Dwight needed some helpers and two valuable people came into his life to help with the Sunday school. First of all Emma Revell, who came from a wealthy family that had recently moved from London to Chicago and then a man named John Farwell came along. Farwell was a successful businessman who was beginning to accumulate his fortune. Farwell was also elected the superintendent of the Northfield Market Mission Sunday School.

Finally, Dwight realized God's calling for full-time Christian service and left the business world. He again found himself homeless and eating very little. Soon he began to sleep in a YMCA and served as their janitor to earn his right to sleep there. Dwight's confidence in his decision that it was completely what God wanted him to do made Farwell respect him even more, which led to his financial backing.

Phase III – Practical Theology

YMCA

Living and working in one of the Chicago YMCA's brought many opportunities for Dwight to meet with other Christians. With people noticing Dwight's zeal for the winning souls, he soon became in full-time service in the YMCA as their city missionary and librarian. However, they did not have enough money to pay him except for some compensation for activities he performed on their behalf. This eventually led to the YMCA's sponsorship of the Sunday school mission. Another development in Dwight's life was his marriage to his ministry partner in the Sunday school mission, Emma Revell.

Emma basically took over the Sunday school ministry during the Civil War because Dwight began helping with the war effort. He recruited soldiers and then when a camp was established outside Chicago he saw a great need. Dwight began to minister to the thousands of soldiers in Camp Douglas and even started a Christian Association Tent for the soldiers. When wounded soldiers began to return to the camp from battle, Moody's ministry changed with the change in attitude of the soldiers. He also took a stand and preached to the prisoners of war that were brought to the camp under guard.

Dwight even ran into some controversy with his way of ministering to the sick and dying. He had the idea that if a man was saved there was no need to waste too much time talking to him when there were dying men who did not know Christ. Some people felt that Moody's pointing out the sin in soldiers' lives and even comparing them to the thief on the cross so that they could be saved was unpatriotic. But Dwight simply ignored the criticism and went ahead doing the same ministry.

Dwight also got to know General O. O. Howard who was a wonderful Christian general. General Howard and Dwight began having services in the camp and then also on the front. Through Gen. Howard, Dwight visited the frontlines nine times. Gen. Howard became a very important man after the war because he was known for his compassion for ex-slaves. He became the head of the Freedman's Bureau and later on the president and founder of Howard University.

Phase IV – Ministry Maturing

Home Front Ministry

Dwight started his first church because of the overwhelming numbers of children and adults attending the Sunday school mission's meetings. The Illinois Street Church opened its doors and many people came to hear the gospel message. Now Dwight Moody not only had his YMCA and Sunday school ministries, but he was also the senior pastor of a fast growing church. With this new ministry came more responsibility, which did not slack off, it only grew.

Soon after he opened the church, the YMCA of Chicago voted him the president of the Chicago association. Dwight made the best of the opportunity and he began to raise money for a new YMCA building. The need for a new building was great because of the many new Christians in Chicago partly because of Dwight's other ministries. The building was completed and through his role as president he developed many different ministries for the sick and poor in the YMCA.

With the stresses of having so many ministries going on at the same time the Moodys did not really have time to think. Emma soon became sick after the birth of her child and then the death of her father drove her even further into sickness. To help relieve Emma's burden, she was taken out of her ministry role which meant that Dwight had even more to do. Soon he began to show signs of an impending collapse and with Emma's development of a serious cough a doctor prescribed that a trip might help. Soon the Moodys were headed on a sea voyage to England to help both of them ease their sickness.

Abroad Ministries

In England, Dwight hoped to seek out several key people and conferences that were going on. He attended a Sunday school convention in London, which opened up some speaking engagements for him while in England. He was also able to hear Charles Spurgeon, one of his personal heroes, preach several times. Another hero Dwight had the opportunity to see was George Mueller. The two had some time to talk and Dwight was able to ask many questions of the wiser gentleman. From Mueller, Dwight learned some valuable lessons on how to study the Bible.

Also while in England, Dwight met a man named Henry Moorhouse. The man was impressed with Dwight and wanted to travel back with the Moodys to speak for Dwight in Chicago. Dwight did not especially want the man who looked like a boy to speak because he was not sure if he had the gift. However, a few months after returning home the Moodys received noticed that Moorhouse was in America and soon after that he came to Chicago. Moorhouse was allowed to speak and his messages were a great success.

Home Front Ministries

Dwight had built a new building for the YMCA and had named it Farwell Hall after his friend and partner in ministry John Farwell. Only three months after it had been built a fire destroyed it completely. Rather than be depressed by the situation, Dwight immediately began to raise funds to build a new building. A few months later, a new building was under construction and its completion became a symbol of pride.

In 1871, a few years after the YMCA fire, Dwight was preaching in his church when the city fire bell was heard. As fires were common no one paid too much attention to it until they noticed it was not stopping. A fire that night and the next day destroyed 18,000 buildings including all Dwight had built, even his house. Again, not letting the fire get him down, he quickly set off to raise funds to help construct temporary buildings for churches and other ministries that were destroyed.

Aboard Ministries

Upon returning to Great Britain, Dwight was asked to speak in a church, which he reluctantly accepted. During his evening sermon the Spirit moved and the whole church accepted Christ. This was the beginning of a ten-day revival in that church which changed hundreds of lives. He then set up speaking engagements for the next year to continue this revivalist evangelism. His second trip back for the revivals was a repeat of the first with hundreds of sinners saved to Christ.

While in England, Dwight also began to develop future Christian leaders. He did so by taking earnest Christians looking for more in terms of service and placing them into a supervised ministry setting. By being able to watch them in action, Dwight would gradually increase their amount of responsibility until they could continue the ministry on their own.

Phase V – Developing Education

First Schools

While in Northfield visiting Dwight had the vision to create a new strategy dealing with schools. His strategy was unlike any other before and had five main interconnected points. Armed with this new strategy, Dwight looked for different ways to begin these ministries. The first way he saw was in the developing of a seminary for women. The seminary was well thought out and well staffed. The ministry was a success when the expected eight girls attending the opening semester was more than doubled with twenty-five girls showing up.

After the girls' seminary was launched, people began to ask for a school for boys to attend. Mount Hermon was started and accepted boys of all ages. Soon the problem developed of having so many boys of different ages that the school began to limit the acceptance age to sixteen and over. The curriculum for the boys' school also changed making the school a college preparatory school.

Bible Institute

Then Moody had the great vision of beginning a Bible institute in Chicago for more working people. The institute was to develop students who wanted to be pastor's assistants, workers in urban ministry, foreign missionaries, and English Bible teachers. The need for these people was great. The institute, although it had its bumps to begin with, began to grow in its mission to train people for ministry. Unlike the other schools Dwight had begun, he maintained a hands-on approach and even developed new programs for the institution.

Phase VI – Finishing Well

Innovations

Dwight had a passion for publications and the spread of Christian literature into the hand of those who needed it. He saw that there was a great need for religious material to edify Christians and help them mature in the faith. Many Christians could not afford to buy literature. Dwight brought his brother-in-law, Fleming Revell into full-time Christian service and Revell began to publish Christian material. Later, Dwight had another plan to try to get more materials into Christians' hands. While he would promote the books, Revell would design works done in the popular style, by well-known authors, with undenominational content, for a low price, and done with high quality workmanship. Moody basically ended up carrying Revell's company with his own works because so many people bought his works.

Another innovation that Dwight saw in ministry was that of starting Christian conferences. He had seen Christian conferences in England and there were conferences in America, but the vision God laid on his heart was for something different. He began by having conferences in Northfield. The conferences would have many people come from all over the world, and would deal mostly with the Spirit's work. Dwight also began to hold college student conferences, which turned into a big success. Soon there were about seven to eight thousand people traveling through Northfield for just the conferences.

Foundations Era:
Death of Father
Formative Encounter: Family Tragedy
Age: 4

Incident

While Edwin Moody was doing some construction work, he suddenly experienced a severe pain, which made him leave work early. As he arrived home and made his way toward his bed, he collapsed to his knees and fell dead in front of his wife, Betsy Moody.

Betsy Moody was eight months pregnant at the time of her husband's death and Edwin had acquired a significant amount of debt. As soon as Edwin died, Betsy instructed her oldest son Isaiah to hide Edwin's masonry tools and their cow's young calf. Before anything else could be hidden, creditors came and took almost every possession from the home. Their home was basically all that was left and simply for the reason she had the right to keep it. However, Betsy had to make the mortgage payments that her husband had agreed upon.

A month after Edwin's death, Betsy gave birth to twins, a boy and a girl. This meant that she now had nine children to raise, all under the age of thirteen. Many people tried to persuade Betsy to break up the family and put the older children in institutions or with other families. Betsy refused to let her family break apart and a few neighbors and family members came to her aid.

Interpretive Comments

The death of his father instilled in D. L. Moody a fear of death that he held for many years. His mother's determination to hold the family together at all costs came to be the source of closeness he had with his mother in later years. His mother also showed Moody values on the importance of family.

Also, the loving support he saw from his uncle remained with him as a fond memory of these younger years.

Spiritual Application

God can use tragic events in one's life to bring about great things. Always look for a great promise from God in the midst of tragedy. The promise might not be visible for some time, but eventually it will be revealed.

Foundations Era:
Religious Interest
Formative Encounter: Model of Ministry
Age: 4-6

Incident

Soon after her husband's death, Reverend Oliver Everett the pastor of the Northfield Unitarian Church befriended Betsy Moody. Everett was one of the few people who encouraged Betsy Moody to keep her family together. He told her to trust in God for strength in bringing up the children alone. Everett also promised to help her with the children's educations and general necessities. The reverend provided the Moody family with counsel and material assistance, for both of which the family had great need. It seemed as though, through his kindness and counsel, Reverend Everett pointed Betsy Moody to God.

Soon after their father's burial, the older children were enrolled in Sunday school. Only a few weeks later the whole family was baptized. Then on January 1, 1843, Betsy Moody became a member of Reverend Everett's Northfield Unitarian Church.

Interpretive Comments

Reverend Oliver Everett had a profound impact on Dwight L. Moody's life. Everett was one of the few people to encourage Betsy Moody to keep her family together rather than split the children up to save money. Not only did he do that, but he also supported the family financially and personally. Everett also showed Betsy to look toward God for her strength and helped guide her into the church. Through Everett's example he showed the whole family some of God's attributes including love, mercy, and compassion. A lesson the good pastor undoubtedly taught D.L. Moody was from Sunday school. Every week, Everett would encourage the children to go into their neighborhoods and find every child they could and bring them for a time of fellowship, praise, and teaching.

Spiritual Application

One should never underestimate the power that being an example of Christ can have in someone's life. Showing Godly attributes such as love, mercy, and compassion can change someone's life completely or it could simply plant the seed for later cultivation.

Foundations Era:
Isaiah's Desertion
Formative Encounter Ac: Family Tragedy
Age: 7

Incident

In 1843, the oldest son of Betsy Moody, Isaiah, disappeared mysteriously. Isaiah was only when he disappeared. The oldest son, (now that their father Edwin had passed away), was the man of the family and was expected to look after family affairs. Betsy Moody was counting on Isaiah to help her raise the other children and keep the family together. Also, Isaiah being old enough to work would allow him to earn some income to help the family financially.

Isaiah devastated the family with his disappearance. He never spoke of leaving, said good-bye, or hinted of his plan. This disappearance was thought of as his death, but of course no one was sure. Betsy Moody was probably the most devastated with evidence of that seen in the fact that her hair turned gray in a matter of weeks after Isaiah's desertion. Nothing was heard of Isaiah until thirteen years later when he finally came back home to Northfield.

Interpretive Comments

Through Isaiah's desertion of the family, which was thought of as a mysterious death, and the death of their father Edwin, Dwight L. Moody had a childhood fear of death. Isaiah's desertion left the family with fewer resources to provide for material needs and therefore the family remained in poverty. D.L. Moody often spoke of joy of these early years of poverty because it made him appreciate what he did have even more.

Spiritual Application

God provides for us even when it seems as though there is no way out. Also, instead of complaining about what we do not have we should celebrate what God has given us.

Foundations Era:
Compassionate Teacher
Formative Encounter Ad: Childhood Guidance
Age: Childhood

Incident

The Moody children were enrolled in a one-room schoolhouse, which they only attended sporadically because most of them had to work to earn money for the family. One year, a new teacher came to teach at the school. On her first day she did two things that shocked the students. First, she opened the class with a prayer, which the instructor before her had not done. Second, she announced that unlike before, she would not enforce discipline by using a whip to flog the students when they were misbehaving.

Within a few days, Dwight Moody had broken the rules and was told to stay after school. Half expecting her to pull out a whip she surprisingly sat down and told Dwight that she loved every one of the boys and she was not going to whip anyone. While she talked to Dwight she wept, which broke Dwight's rebellious spirit. After that Dwight kept the other boys in line with the rules.

Interpretive Comments

This brilliant teacher won the students by her grace, not her power with the whip. She also brought prayer into the school, which reinforced where her compassion for the boys was coming from. In later years, Dwight mentioned this incident in many of his sermons and never forgot her compassion.

Spiritual Application

Being an example of Christ's compassion and grace can have enormous effect on people's lives.

Foundations Era:
Good Samaritan
Formative Encounter Ae: Divine Contact
Age: 10

Incident

When Dwight was only ten, his brother Luther, eleven, went to Greenfield to do chores for a family. Luther was very homesick and wanted Dwight to come to Greenfield with him. That fall, Luther came home and told Dwight that he had found a family that he could do chores for in Greenfield. Reluctantly, Dwight went with Luther the thirteen miles over to Greenfield where he stayed with a childless couple.

After a week of doing chores for the family, Dwight became very homesick and went to see his brother at the house where he was boarded. Dwight informed his brother that he was going home because he was too homesick to stay. Luther got Dwight to go with him on a walk through town looking in store windows because they did not have enough money to buy anything. Along came a man who noticed Dwight was a new boy in town. When the man stopped to talk to Dwight he told him about their Father in heaven and that He loved him so much that He sent His only Son to die for us. The old man then told Dwight the whole story of the cross in about five minutes. Then the man put his hand in his pocket and gave Dwight a bright, new cent. Dwight later recalled that act of kindness as taking all of his homesickness away.

Interpretive Comments

In later sermons, Dwight said that at the time he thought that the old man was God and how he felt from that moment on that he had a friend. His brother Luther knew the old man would give Dwight a cent when he saw that he was a new boy in town. The old man gave every new boy a cent. Luther helped Dwight with his homesickness by directing him to the man that would perform an unforgettable act of kindness in Dwight's life.

Spiritual Application

Dwight was able to see the face of God in that old man when he gave him the bright, new cent. The act of kindness with the story of the cross and of God's love left the lasting impression in Dwight's life. Being the face of God for other people is all it takes to open the door for God's love to shine through to them.

Foundations Era:
Conversion
Formative Encounter Ba: Divine Contact
Age: 18

Incident

Soon after leaving Northfield for a more exciting life in the metropolis of Boston, Dwight Moody found himself homeless and jobless. His uncle Samuel hired young Dwight as a sales clerk and found him a room in a house on the stipulation that Dwight must go to Sunday school and church. Dwight then began attending the Mount Vernon Congregational Church under his uncle's guidance. Dwight was willing to commit to this agreement but Dwight immensely disliked the place. He admired and respected Dr. Kirk, the pastor of the church, but found it hard to understand his messages.
On Dwight's first day in the Sunday school class the teacher, Edward Kimball, asked all the students to turn to the book of John in the Bible. Dwight did not know where the book of John was located and was fruitlessly thumbing through the book. Noticing the effort being put into the task Kimball gave Dwight his own Bible and continued about the lesson. After this incident Dwight had tremendous respect for Edward Kimball for saving him from an embarrassing situation.
On April 18, 1855, Edward Kimball was preparing for his Sunday school lesson for the next day and he felt an urge to talk to Dwight. Immediately Kimball headed out the door to the shoe store Dwight worked in. When Kimball arrived at the store he went and simply told Dwight about Christ's love for him and the love Christ wanted in return. After a few more words, Dwight gave himself and his life to Christ.

Interpretive Comments

This conversion experience and the obedience of Edward Kimball to the Holy Spirit is what God used to awaken Moody to the reality of the spiritual world. This experience brought young Dwight into a personal relationship with Jesus Christ and brought his spiritual side to life.

Spiritual Application

Obedience to the Spirit's calling permits great accomplishments for the Kingdom. When the Spirit calls, move.

Inner-Life Growth:
Mentors
Formative Encounter Aa: Divine Contacts
Age: 19

Incident

Soon after Dwight's move to Chicago in 1856, he found work and a room in a local shoe store. Dwight's ambition for wealth led to him being very exact and economical with his spending habits and made him a zealous and tireless worker. However, his ambition for wealth and his new yet vibrant spirituality were in conflict. Young Dwight felt the need now to speak up during church meetings and to be more involved in church activities.

This led to an invitation from a Christian woman for free lodging and meals at her house if he would give up the shoe trade and go into full-time Christian work. Dwight however, did not want to give up his employment. Towards the end of 1856 a revival swept through Chicago and his landlady, Mrs. Phillips or "Mother" Phillips as she was called, began to nurture the young convert. Mother Phillips taught Dwight the importance of prayer, Bible study, scripture memorization, and disciple making. Mother Phillips also pointed Dwight in the direction of the many rescue missions that had been started for the poor by the revival atmosphere in Chicago.

As Dwight ministered on the streets of Chicago performing evangelistic work he ran into another man, twice his age, doing the same thing. This man was J.B. Stillson. Stillson began to mentor the young enthusiastic Christian in how to be a soul physician to those suffering from poverty as well as people in hospitals and prisons. They also recruited children for about twenty different mission Sunday schools because they felt better leaving children in the hands of teachers rather than doing that work themselves.

Interpretive Comments

"Mother" Phillips and J.B. Stillson served as Dwight's spiritual parents giving the young, uneducated Christian a foundation he could hold onto throughout his ministry. During this time of mentoring, Dwight learned the importance of prayer before he attempted to perform any type of ministry seeking the Lord's blessing on it. Also, he developed a personal devotion life that is key to a growing Christian's life.

Spiritual Application

A strong foundation in the basic pillars of prayer, scripture study, and mentoring create a firm stronghold to help any Christian perform his or her calling in ministry.

Inner-Life Growth:
Sunday School Ministry
Formative Encounter Ab: Ministry Tasks
Age: 21

Incident

Dwight found himself being drawn more and more to children's ministry. The children's ministry he began to work with was among the children living in the most undignified conditions where most missionaries to the poor refused to go. The area Dwight's ministry took form was in the worst district of Chicago called "the Sands" or sometimes, "Little Hell." The children of this area were usually illiterate and came from homes with only one parent who usually was an alcoholic or drug addict.

Dwight entered the Sands with confidence, knowing that God had armed him for this ministry to rescue the children. The disability he had among proper company in the elite circles of Chicago due to his lack of education made him well suited for the task he took on with teaching the children of the Sands. In 1858, Moody rented out a vacant, worn down old saloon and turned it into a "Sabbath School" for the little children.

With Dwight's dynamic personality and unusual method of handing out candy to any child who would come to the meeting; his meetings soon became very popular. Every session included singing, prayer, Bible readings, stories, and at the same time, fights, screaming, and laughter. Even though this Sunday school may have not looked or sounded like traditional schools, children came in increasing numbers to take part in the sessions.

Interpretive Comments

Dwight's acceptance of this role of ministry led to a developing of his calling of evangelistic work. This is displayed in his going out into the slums of Chicago where other Christians refused to go because of the persecution Christians often experienced when they entered with a condemning message. Dwight's message of hope and his willingness to take a risk by reaching out to the children of the Sands is what jump started his leadership in ministry.

Spiritual Application

Armed with knowledge of scripture and confidence of the Spirit's guidance a Christian can accomplish extraordinary feats. Without knowledge of scripture and the Spirit's confidence, Christian work is fruitless. In order to win souls for Christ, these applications must be present.

Inner-Life Growth:
Valuable Workers
Formative Encounter Ac: Divine Contacts
Age: 21

Incident

The first important person who entered into Dwight's life as a valuable worker was Ms. Emma Revell. Emma came from a somewhat wealthy family who had recently relocated to Chicago from London, England. Emma brought a far better education than Moody and also had the experience of living in a stable and cultured family life. After her own personal conversion experience in the revival in Chicago in 1857, Emma and Dwight met at a service where he was speaking on his ministry to the poor. After Dwight moved the Sunday school from the old saloon to the North Market Hall, Emma became a regular teacher of Sands ministry.

The second valuable worker Dwight Moody had respond to his plea for help was John V. Farwell. Being able to read and write well enough, Farwell was able to attend Mount Morris Seminary during the winter terms from 1841 to 1844. Farwell then came to Chicago with dreams of wealth in his head. Soon enough, he became a partner of a firm, which within two years bore only his name and his annual sales were more than $100,000. Moody and Farwell met through a Sunday school class they both were enrolled in and Moody's example of Christianity shook Farwell. Soon afterward, Farwell became a financial support system for Dwight's visions for the children's ministry. Farwell was then invited to speak to the children and before he knew it he had been elected by the children and Dwight as the superintendent of the Northfield Market Mission Sunday School.

Interpretive Comments

Dwight Moody would not have been able to develop the Northfield Market Mission Sunday School without the support, both physical and financial from both Emma Revell and John Farwell. The popularity of the school grew so much that their regular attendance was close to 2,000 by the end of 1860. Also, President-elect Abraham Lincoln visited the well-known school in November on his first visit to Chicago. This important visitor brought status and respectability to Dwight, but Emma and John were attracted to Dwight's tenderness and love for souls.

Spiritual Application

Dwight Moody was able to show to both Emma Revell and John Farwell the importance of putting ones faith in action while sanctifying one's heart before the Lord. The most important aspect Moody displayed was Christ's unconditional love for the lost

Inner-Life Growth:
Soul Struggle
Formative Encounter Ad: Obedience Check
Age: 23

Incident

Dwight began to notice a struggle going on within his soul. He enjoyed many things, but the commitment he had to ministry made some of those things burdensome. A conflict of his will to the calling of God was taking place. Moody noticed that it seemed whenever the Lord was calling him into higher Christian service his own will was fighting against that of God. In 1860, Moody felt God's Spirit calling him to leave the business world and enter into the ministry full-time. This initial struggle marks back to the time when "Mother" Phillips asked him to go into full-time Christian service but he did not want to leave the money. The struggle was even harder for Dwight because he had begun to earn more money than he had ever earned before. Not only was his bank account growing, but also Dwight was experiencing the fulfillment of having the recognition of others in his success commercially.

Once Dwight made the decision to follow God's will for his life, he never looked back. Immediately he gave notice to his employers and told his close friends of his decision. Dwight was then out on the streets spending many nights on park benches and dining on cheese and crackers. Eventually he found a room in a YMCA and he worked as a janitor there. Many people urged the once financially growing and successful Moody to go back to the business world but he refused to even think of their idea. Dwight's fervent attitude once again opened Farwell's eyes and he saw growth in Moody. Farwell again decided to provide Dwight's financial backing so that he would never have a need for any necessity.

Interpretive Comments

The world called for Dwight Moody and he was answering the call successfully. He was well on his way to becoming a very successful businessman with many people looking up his success. However, Dwight decided to not answer the world's call for his life but rather the Lord's call. After enduring the initial testing of his faithfulness but the trials of no food, shelter, and friends questioning his judgment, Moody then was set for entering God's full-time service.

Spiritual Application

Following God's calling on ones life is the most important decision anyone can make. Choosing to put aside financial gains or whatever may be one's own personal dreams and taking up the cross that Christ has asked us to bear is what the Christian life is truly about.

Practical Theology:
YMCA
Formative Encounter Aa: Sphere of Influence
Age: 24

Incident

Dwight Moody found the Young Men's Christian Association to be a valuable school of practical theology. The YMCA provided many ways of performing evangelistic work for Dwight when many churches and missions thought of him as unqualified. He first began to work with the YMCA during the revival that swept through Chicago in 1857, but as time went on he became more and more involved. However, his involvement was not in the power structure that ran the YMCA, but rather Dwight took on jobs that no one else wanted. He would perform janitorial duties, prepare fires on cold days so it would be warm when people arrived, and also he would roam the streets looking for young men to come to the prayer meetings.

Once Dwight decided to follow God's calling and go into full-time ministry he became the YMCA's city missionary and librarian, while unofficially serving as both their janitor and superintendent. While he served in all these various positions he was working for free because the YMCA did not have enough funds to pay him. Dwight did receive a free place to sleep, which saved him from paying the cost of rent. He also received some compensation for activities he performed on the YMCA's behalf. The greatest thing the YMCA did was to assume official sponsorship of Moody's North Market Hall Mission and Sunday School in 1861. This allowed Dwight the use of official letterhead and gave him more credibility.

Interpretive Comments

While the YMCA did not have the money to pay Dwight Moody for his incredible service to their organization, both the YMCA and Moody received contributions from one another. The YMCA received a very loyal, energetic evangelist whose primary concern was for lost souls to come to know Christ. Dwight's care and concern for the poor was also in line with part of the YMCA's core goal. From the YMCA, Moody received an official sponsorship for his mission school. More importantly for him personally was the fact that the well-known businessmen in leadership of the YMCA began to call him "Brother Moody," which removed the title of Crazy Moody that had been circulating in various circles.

Spiritual Application

Often times it may seem like foolishness to people when Christians enter full-time Christian service.

Practical Theology:
Marriage
Formative Encounter Ab: Destiny Preparation
Age: 25

Incident

Dwight Moody was almost as obsessed with Emma Revell as he was with the Christian ministry to lost souls. Since he recruited her to be a part of the mission Sunday school, his affection and respect for her had grown stronger. Dwight felt that marriage was a part of the calling God had laid on his life and that marriage and his full-time ministry calling were to go hand in hand. From the time the couple was engaged they took every opportunity they could to minister together. Emma was his right hand in the mission Sunday school and often helped him with the ministry to the poor. From now on, if Dwight Moody was in ministry that meant that Emma Moody was also.

Interpretive Comments

Dwight and Emma Moody's marriage was no surprise to anyone that knew the couple because of how well they worked in ministry together. Everyone could also see that they were obviously devoted to one another, their marriage however was merely a reflection of their even greater devotion to God and the calling He had on their lives. This also reveals Dwight Moody's thoughts on women in ministry as he had no trouble sending Emma off to do ministry for God's Kingdom.

Spiritual Application

Dwight and Emma Moody while having a great ministry together also set a wonderful example of how a Christian marriage should look. The two would spend their lives supporting each other in ministry and in life.

Practical Theology:
72nd Illinois Volunteers
Formative Encounter Ba: Ministry Task
Age: 24

Incident

As the Civil War began, President Lincoln called for 75,000 volunteers and Chicago had an overwhelming response. To help out with the mobilization of the war effort, the Chicago YMCA volunteered their assistance in raising money and organizing companies. About six hundred men were put into service through the YMCA. Dwight Moody helped with all of these arrangements for the various companies and regiments that had been formed. Later, he was placed as the chairman of the committee for devotional meetings to feed the spiritual needs of the fighting soldiers.

The 72nd Illinois Volunteer Regiment was organized and Moody as a representative of the YMCA and a friend of many men in the regiment came daily to read scripture, preach and pray with them. The 72nd had been moved south of Chicago to Camp Douglas, and while many men tried to persuade Dwight to join them as their chaplain he eventually declined as many other regiments were coming to Camp Douglas and he saw the greater need. Camp Douglas became the largest city in Illinois with thousands of men drinking and prostitution moving down from the city to fulfill the men's sexual lusts. Dwight realized that he would be able to help more if he were free to move around instead of assigned to one regiment.

Dwight then had the vision of establishing a sort of makeshift church. He started by printing thousands of hymnals that were passed out to the soldiers and then thousands of Bibles, tracts and other gospel booklets. He began to preach from around eight to ten times a day to the men of Camp Douglas, and from that he established the Christian Association Tent. The Christian Association Tent had available religious material as well as writing utensils to allow the soldiers to write home to their families.

Interpretive Comments

Dwight Moody had the vision to not attach himself to one regiment, which would require him to minister to only a hundred men when he had the ability to minister to thousands. Seeing the men falling into sin in their idleness waiting for the call of battle, Moody knew that something had to be done. His vision for a Christian association dedicated to preaching the gospel, and to the spiritual nurturing the souls of the soldiers, and encouraging the men to live morally was a huge step to take from simply speaking to a hundred or so men. Taking the risk to step out on faith to fulfill the perceived need is what made this action so great.

Spiritual Application

Dwight Moody is now learning to look for the larger picture of what the needs of the people are and not simply see what is directly in front of him. The Spirit is enabling him to see the need of the thousands of men in Camp Douglas. With the Spirit's power, a leader can recognize where to go and what to do. With faith, a leader can fulfill what he or she sees as that need.

Practical Theology:
Changing Ministry
Formative Encounter Bb: Spiritual Authority
Age: 24-28

Incident

With Union troops on the advance in southern territory, the needs of the men were different. Therefore, two large changes came about in Dwight Moody's ministry. First of all, nine thousand rebel soldiers that had been taken prisoner were now placed under guard at Camp Douglas. As many Chicagoans became nervous with the possibilities of having so many prisoners so close to the city, Moody on the other hand saw this as an opportunity. Within a few days of the prisoners' arrival, Dwight had already rounded up volunteers to counsel and pray with the prisoners, and he began to preach. From this, thousands of Confederate soldiers experienced love and compassion from their enemy.

The second change came from the condition of the soldiers. At the beginning, Union soldiers were healthy, fit, and happy men but now the men were wounded, sick, and dying lying in makeshift hospitals near the different battle sites. Soon, Dwight became personally linked with the troops under General Grant throughout the remainder of the war. He traveled to the front lines to minister to the soldiers, both fit and sick. The Union forces experienced a significant blow in April 1862 with 13,000 causalities in two days.

Interpretive Comments

The experience left Dwight Moody drained physically and emotionally. The whole time he was ministering with the troops he was trying to maintain his ministry with the Mission Sunday school and his outreach to Chicago's poor. However, Moody was able to adapt his ministry successfully to the needs of the people he was ministering to. Without doing so, he would have been left behind as the times and people changed around him.

Spiritual Application

Dwight Moody's faith during these years reached great heights. He saw God's faithfulness to him recognizing it was the same God of the Old and New Testaments. He also demonstrated the truth that God's love is not for one side of an army or the other. His love and compassion for the Confederate soldiers placed at Camp Douglas shows how Christians are supposed to love their enemy, not hate them.

Practical Theology:
Ministry Controversy
Formative Encounter Bc: Controversy
Age: 26

Incident

Christians did not always appreciate Dwight Moody's zealous search for souls on the home front. A spirited debate arose on a steam ship concerning how Moody conducted his ministry to the sick, wounded, and dying soldiers. Moody's idea of this ministry first of all was to find out if the man was a believer, if so, Dwight recommended not staying too long with him because the soldier was already safe. If the man was not a believer he was to be converted.

Many Christians thought that this idea was wrong because the first concern of these fighting men was to make them comfortable, to calm their nerves not waken their souls. The idea that trying to convert a dying soldier by pointing out his sins and his need to convert was somewhat unpatriotic. Many Christians of the time saw patriotism as a form of piety and dying for one's country was a way of getting into heaven. Moody took this criticism very lightly because many people did not understand fully orthodox Christian theology. Instead, Dwight went right on speaking to each soldier seeking the salvation their souls.

Interpretive Comments

This controversy is the first mentioned controversy concerning Dwight Moody's ministry. While the controversy itself is somewhat trivial, the issue shows how the public viewed evangelism to soldiers, which was Moody's primary concern during the war. It also shows how naïve the general Christian population was to issues of Christian theology.

Spiritual Application

Dwight Moody's ability to take criticism and continue in ministry is how all Christians should react to such things. Criticism is helpful to be able to step back and see how others view your ministry. However, criticism must not change the ministry God has given a leader to perform, unless the Spirit moves the leader to adapt according to the criticism.

Practical Theology:
O. O. Howard
Formative Encounter Bd: Divine Contact
Age: 27

Incident

General Oliver Otis Howard was a Christian soldier who saw a great deal of action. In the beginning of his career, Howard was a controversial commander because he allowed his Christian faith to influence his soldiering. Christian soldiers under his command loved him, but those who had nothing to do with his faith criticized him. During the war, his concern for former slaves earned him more criticism from his men and also his compassion of the noncombatants in the South did not sit well with many who were practicing open pillaging and destroying civilian property.

Moody and Howard met in Cleveland, Tennessee where General Howard and his troops were part of General Sherman's army. Howard and Moody decided to begin services for the soldiers which were to be held both in the camp during the day and in the town churches at night. General Howard even spoke at one of these services and had a large response to his message. Once the war was over, Howard began to speak at various meetings and conferences Moody set up. While Howard never left the army, he became a lay pastor and Bible teacher.

Because of General Howard's care and compassion for ex-slaves during the war, President Lincoln gave him the role of leading the Bureau of Refugees, Freedmen, and Abandoned Lands. Upon Lincoln's death, President Johnson made Howard the head of the Freedman's Bureau. Moody never took part in the Bureau's work, but he did find many workers to help Howard in its cause. In the end, Howard founded and later became the president of a university for black men and women, which now bears his name, Howard University.

Interpretive Comments

Howard and Moody's relationship grew to great heights over the years with each contributing to the reciprocal friendship. From General Howard, Moody learned a great deal about how to lead educational institutions. Howard also taught Moody the delicate and complicated issues surrounding race relations of the time. Moody allowed General Howard to become a lay preacher and conference speaker to many of his people. Whenever Dwight Moody had the chance, he called on General Howard to preach and speak to people.

Spiritual Application

God brings together certain people to allow his grand design to be fulfilled. This relationship between two men shows how God used both to fulfill his ultimate plan. General Howard's faithfulness and fulfillment of his mission is also another example of why Christians should not bow down to criticism to a God given ministry.

Ministry Maturing:
Illinois Street Church
Formative Encounter Aa: Prayer Challenge
Age: 28

Incident

During the early years of the Civil War, the Mission Sunday school Moody had founded had begun to decline in attendance as his attention was diverted elsewhere. Upon his marriage to Emma, the school had a renewed spirit and soon attendance had reached an all time high. With the mission school's attendance soaring, Emma along with others began to pray for what God wanted them to do next with this ministry. Through this prayer it was realized that they needed $20,000 to purchase a lot on a corner in the heart of the North Side poverty. In February 1864, a large brick building stood on that corner that had a 1,500 seat auditorium, several classrooms, a small office and a library.

Once it opened, around one thousand children and teens along with three hundred adults came every Sunday to the Illinois Street Hall. As Dwight had been sending the children to different churches as they had the need, it began to be obvious that this was no longer going to do. In late 1864, the Moodys called local pastors to join them in prayer about beginning a union church, because only such a church could minister to the people who came to the mission school. After much prayer, the Illinois Street Church was dedicated on December 30, 1864. In 1865, Dwight Moody had an independent evangelical church with the most aggressive evangelistic program in Chicago.

Interpretive Comments

With Moody's attention being diverted because of the Civil War, he left his mission Sunday school in the hands of his wife, Emma. In her hands, she turned the falling school into a thriving place. Through prayer, Emma and others realized the need for a new school building, which ended up being used also as a new church with Dwight as the senior pastor. By asking God what he held in store for the school, he revealed his greater plan of opening a new church for the poverty-stricken people of the North Side of Chicago.

Spiritual Application

This demonstrates the power that prayer holds when people ask what next God will show them. The Moodys' faithfulness to follow the vision God gave them is what allowed for such great advances in their ministry.

Ministry Maturing:
Presidency
Formative Encounter Ab: Authority Insights
Age: 28

Incident

Soon after the Illinois Street Church had begun holding regular Sunday morning meetings, the YMCA of Chicago asked Dwight Moody to become their next president. Dwight Moody was seen as the best candidate for the job mostly because of his ability to raise building funds quickly and the YMCA needed a new building. This need for a new facility in the Chicago YMCA was pertinent mostly because of Moody's ministry in Camp Douglas during the war. This plus his enthusiasm for evangelism, love and passion for children, and his unique ability to recruit and employ volunteers made him perfect for the job.

Dwight kept evangelism as the primary mission of the YMCA and used Bible teaching for adults as a secondary ministry. Dwight also began some social programs and under his leadership the YMCA distributed $25,325.38 worth of relief in the way of bread, clothing, and coal in 1867. Also, Chicago had many young women coming to seek employment, and these girls were often taken advantage of or forced into prostitution. To combat this, the YMCA started a boarding house for young working girls to give them a wholesome place to live to keep them from getting swept away by this lifestyle. They also teamed with Chicago Theological Seminary and Hahnemann Medical College to train people to treat those stricken in the cholera epidemic. The YMCA also began printing a religious periodical *Heavenly Things* that contained inspirational stories.

Interpretive Comments

It was later said that Moody's influence on the Chicago YMCA left such a lasting imprint on the association that his ideas continued to dominate the program long after he himself had left. He was very insightful looking beyond the norm and starting social programs that were unheard of in that time in history.

With all the good that he did for the YMCA of Chicago, it seems perhaps that there was a bit of spiritual immaturity on Moody's part for his taking on this role.

Spiritual Application

Dwight Moody was led by the Spirit to complete an amazing, lasting work in the Chicago YMCA. His leadership vision began ministries that touched innumerable lives and possibly planted the seed of the Spirit in thousands of souls for later cultivation.

Ministry Maturing:
Personal Trouble
Formative Encounter Ac: Ministry Conflict
Age: 29

Incident

With the work load pilling up, both Dwight and Emma Moody were showing distressing signs of emotional breakdowns. In the last weeks before Richmond fell to the Union troops, Dwight and Emma, who had only recently given birth, headed to the Atlantic coast to be with General Grant's troops. With her baby being born in October 1864 and a sickness that lasted for three months after the birth, the trip was very hard on her. When they returned to Chicago they returned to all the ministries that had to be attended. Then Dwight decided he needed to return to Northfield to visit his mother and he felt it might help Emma's health. Once they arrived in Massachusetts, they received notice that Emma's father was very ill and they left at once to return home. They arrived after her father had passed away and this devastated Emma since she was very close to her father.

To help Emma gain her strength back, she was removed from her ministry tasks, which meant that Dwight had even more to do. Soon he began to show signs of an emotional collapse. He began to be very forgetful, a sign of collapse, and began to overbook himself with engagements. He so overbooked himself in 1866 that he did not make it home for Christmas. Then he began to lose his temper and even once he pushed a man down a small flight of stairs. Dwight repented, asking forgiveness from his congregation and from the man, but the damage was done. To help him with deliverance from this impending collapse, he decided to take a trip. Soon afterwards, Emma developed a cough and her doctor suggested she take a voyage overseas stating that the sea air would be good for her. From this, Dwight and Emma booked a trip to England.

Interpretive Comments

The strain of the busy life that Dwight and Emma led finally began to catch up with them making both of them ill in different ways. Dwight's problems could have grown to be significantly worse if he hadn't decided to take this trip to England. If an emotional collapse had happened it could have ruined his ministry, and probably anymore outbursts of the anger building up in him could have ruined his reputation as well. Dwight's leadership was failing in part because he failed to delegate authority and responsibility to those who were willing and able around him. Had he done so, his and Emma's health would not have declined so and this trip to England would not have been necessary.

Spiritual Application

When full-time ministry is where God calls, one must be very careful to not strain himself or herself to the point of being unhealthy. God gives us the strength to handle what he assigns to us, but we must be smart enough to say no to some opportunities and allow other people to take on the roles.

Ministry Maturing:
England
Formative Encounter Ba: Isolation
Age: 30

Incident

In early 1867, the Moodys set sail for England with the goal of respiratory healing for Emma and a way for Dwight to alleviate his guilt of neglect. However the trip was not completely a vacation for the Moodys as there were several opportunities that Dwight wanted to take advantage of while in England. Upon arriving in England, Dwight headed to a Sunday school convention in London where he was asked to give a report from America. His speech was well received and soon he had engagements piling up. The Moodys visited prayer meetings, YMCA facilities, worship services, and Sunday schools in England, Scotland, and Ireland. Dwight gave a speech at every stop that he could and continued his work with vigor.

Dwight especially wanted to hear London's most famous preacher, Charles Spurgeon, whose biography had a profound impact on Dwight earlier. Finally, he was able to hear him preach and followed Spurgeon wherever he spoke. Also, Dwight was able to meet with George Mueller whose autobiography had also gripped him. As Dwight always did, he assumed the role of student around people who knew more about God and about ministry than he did and he soaked up bits of wisdom from Mueller. Dwight also asked tons of questions to Mueller to discover how he got so much out of scripture and how he became such a wonderful Bible teacher.

Interpretive Comments

Dwight Moody's impact on Britain in 1867 was profound, but his impact was not as great as the influence he received from those he met while there. In meeting some of his heroes, Dwight received invaluable knowledge on various topics, most importantly he learned from Mueller how to read scripture and how to gain more from its reading. Though this isolation may not have been isolation in the truest definition of the word, the trip served to remove Dwight from his ministry setting and allow him to pick up helpful information to further develop his ministry.

Spiritual Application

This chance at renewal is exactly what Dwight needed. Spiritual retreats can serve to rejuvenate weaken spirits and can end in producing greater fruits.

Ministry Maturing:
Henry Moorhouse
Formative Encounter Bb: Influence Challenge
Age: 30

Incident

While the Moodys were still in England, a man from Ireland came to England to hear Dwight preach. After listening to the sermon, the man, who looked like a boy found Dwight and told him that he would come to America to preach for him. Dwight did not want to have the "boy" accompany him and his wife, but God had other plans. Several weeks after the Moodys had returned home they received word that Harry Moorhouse was in America and he wanted to come to Chicago and preach.

Moorhouse arrived in Chicago and Dwight invited him to speak, but the officers of the church were not so sure of this young man. Dwight was headed out of town but left instructions with the officers that depending on how well Moorhouse spoke they could extend his invitation of speaking to last throughout the week. Dwight left Moorhouse in Emma's hands and under the care of the church officers. It turned out that Moorhouse was a huge success and preached from John 3:16 seven sermons in a row using the whole of scripture to show God's love for mankind.

Interpretive Comments

Moorhouse's visit to Chicago had a significant effect on Dwight Moody's life and he was never the same man again. The Holy Spirit used Moorhouse to point out to Moody that God is love and that Christ came to Earth to save sinners. The salvation granted us through Christ is unearned, undeserved, and unrepayable. "Love them into the Kingdom" became a key transformational proclamation of theology to Moody that Moorhouse had left him. Moorhouse also helped change Dwight's whole approach to preaching.

Spiritual Application

God uses the most unlikely people to drastically change our lives. Often times the people who influence our lives the most are those in whom we place no expectations of doing so. Allowing God to use those around us while not prohibiting those who He leads in our direction is the key to gaining the most from Him.

Ministry Maturing:
YMCA Fire
Formative Encounter Ad: Ministry Crisis
Age: 31

Incident

On January 7, just three months after its construction, Farwell Hall burned to the ground. Farwell Hall was a beautiful new building that Moody had led construction of for the Chicago YMCA. The hall and several other neighboring buildings were all destroyed in the catastrophic fire. Not letting crisis ruin him, Moody began collecting funds to rebuild Farwell Hall even before the remains of the old were removed. By April, over half of what was needed to rebuild had been raised and that's when Dwight hit up Cyrus McCormick, the farm equipment tycoon for $50,000, which he graciously agreed to. A few days over a year after it burned, Farwell Hall number two opened its doors anew and became a monument of pride.

Interpretive Comments

This semi-crisis shows how Dwight Moody reacts to crisis situations. Most people would become depressed when a building project that one has been so personally involved in is destroyed. Dwight Moody simply saw what needed to be done to rebuild and began to do so almost as quickly as the building was destroyed.

Spiritual Application

The Lord gives and the Lord takes away. Nothing we own on this earth have we earned, everything has been given. We should not be upset if we lose something because it was never really ours to begin with.

Ministry Maturing:
Trial by Fire
Formative Encounter Ae: Crisis
Age: 34

Incident

Sunday, October 8, 1871, Dwight Moody made his way to Farwell Hall to preach. At the end of his service a fire bell for the city was heard. This sound was not unfamiliar to the people of Chicago because of the numerous fires that plagued the city. However, this night was different; the fire bells continued to ring. Aided by drought like conditions and a strong southwest wind the fire soon turned into an inferno destroying everything in its path. The fire that began on Sunday night took until Tuesday afternoon to put out.

At the end of the horror, this inferno had engulfed four square miles. Over 18,000 buildings were destroyed leaving more than 100,000 people homeless and around one thousand people died. When the damages were totaled, the amount exceeded $200,000,000. Included in the fire's destruction were the Illinois Street Church, the second Farwell Hall, and Moody's own home. In the aftermath of the great loss, the Moody family stayed with Emma's sister outside Chicago. Less than a month after the fire, Moody packed his bags and began to travel to many of the east coast cities in an effort to raise funds for Chicago's churches and missions.

Interpretive Comments

With this fire hitting a little closer to home, Dwight Moody seems a little shaken. With this being the second fire to destroy Farwell Hall and seeing everything he built with his own hands basically destroyed in an instant was devastating. Instead of dwelling on his losses and taking personal time to regroup with his family, Moody quickly returned to a life of fundraising. Through his fundraising efforts many temporary buildings were put up for church meetings across Chicago.

Spiritual Application

Not allowing crises the Devil throws your way to crush you and taking everything that comes your way with the knowledge that God is good is a key to surviving personal losses.

Ministry Maturing:
Britain Revival
Formative Encounter Bc: Obedience Check
Age: 35

Incident

In 1872, Dwight Moody returned to Great Britain to gain a deeper understanding of the scriptures. When Dwight arrived, a preacher, Reverend John Lessey, asked Moody if he would speak on Sunday at his church. While in the morning service the people seemed to be indifferent, the evening service was full of God's Spirit. At the conclusion of the service Dwight asked for those who wished to become Christians to stand to their feet and everyone in the service stood. This response was a surprise to both Moody and Lessey.

The next day Dwight sailed over to Ireland to visit some Bible teachers on the island, but as soon as he reached land he received an urgent message asking him to return to England because there were a number of people seeking God's word. As soon as he got the message, he began his trek back to England and when he arrived he preached and ministered for ten days. During these ten days, four hundred people made confessions of faith and joined Lessey's church.

After this local revival, Dwight realized God leading him to preach, so he began to accept all the invitations to preach. This trip was no longer a personal study trip but became an evangelistic revival trip. As his trip was coming to a close, he set up a series of meetings for a return trip, which he set up for early the next year with a huge response for the Kingdom.

Interpretive Comments

Dwight Moody began the trip to have a personal isolation away from the busy schedule he had at home with ministry so he could have a chance to develop himself further in God's Word. However, once he arrived and reluctantly agreed to preach a couple of sermons the Lord quickly revealed that that was not what God's plan was for Dwight's trip. Moody's willingness to obey God's calling produced hundreds of converts, which in turned touched many more lives.

Spiritual Application

Sometimes God throws us for a loop when he reveals ministry opportunities when we think He has planned us for something else. However, the acceptance of what God asks us to do always produces wonderful things.

Ministry Maturing:
Developing Leaders
Formative Encounter Bd: Destiny Revelation
Age: 38

Incident

During his voyages to Britain one of Dwight Moody's most important contributions was the development of Christian workers and leaders. Dwight's development of such leaders can be seen in his work with two people, Miss Cotton and Mr. Henry Drummond. After meeting such Christians and noticing their willingness to commit to do work for Christ, Dwight would place these would be leaders in a supervised ministry role. Through this setting Dwight could oversee their development and gradually increase their responsibilities until they were ready for their own personal ministries.

Interpretive Comments

Dwight Moody was not interested in his own personal glory in developing others, he simply wanted to see souls won for Christ. The singleness of his purpose allowed him to select, encourage, and develop leaders from people who showed a burden for more training. He loved to elevate others to the foreground while he would disappear in the background. Dwight's belief was that there were others better than him who were coming after him. His belief that God had bigger plans for others is what led him to train others for Christian leadership.

Spiritual Application

Bringing others up in Christ is an invaluable tool to further the Kingdom. No one ever knows exactly what God has in store for a person's life. Therefore all Christians should work to better others in the faith.

Developing Education:
New Strategy
Formative Encounter Aa: Upward Development
Age: 41

Incident

While visiting Northfield for a year, Dwight Moody developed an overall plan he saw the need for to improve his ministry. The plan had five pillars, which were all connected to each other in some way. The first point was the fact that to reach the most people; one had to have an urban strategy. With urbanization beginning, Dwight Moody had the vision to see that to have the most effective ministry possible; one had to minister in urban settings. The second observation Moody developed was that truly effective work must be done in the inquiry room, a very personal work speaking directly to people about Christ face-to-face. Dwight had been running brief training sessions for workers in this aspect, but he found their training to be insufficient.

Dwight's third point in this development strategy was to equip people who were not far removed from the lowest economic level themselves for city mission work. These people needed no college or seminary degree, they simply needed training in evangelism, personal work, the Bible, and basic doctrine. The fourth piece of the strategy was to train missionaries to go into all the corners of the world. The last part of the puzzle was a more sentimental aspect to Dwight himself, but was still connected to the others. That was to help poor children, especially young girls who were trapped in the rural poverty of New England.

Interpretive Comments

This strategy Dwight came up with is certainly a God given vision to develop leaders to win souls for Christ. Moody had the forward thinking to see ahead of the times and see the needs that would develop in city ministry. While he was interested in urban ministry, Dwight did not forget God's command to go into the entire world with his plan to train missionaries to go to all the far reaching corners of the world.

Spiritual Application

God gives people great vision sometimes to see what He wants done for His Kingdom. The key is to pay attention to God when he gives you these pieces of wisdom.

Developing Education:
Northfield Seminary
Formative Encounter Ab: Destiny Fulfillment
Age: 42

Incident

Armed with his new strategy, Dwight Moody began to find ways to implement it. His idea to help girls trapped in the poverty of New England led to the idea to start a seminary in Northfield. Through careful choosing of faculty, staff, and the board of trustees, the school was opened on November 3, 1879. They had projected around eight women coming for that first semester, but to everyone's surprise, twenty-five showed up for the first day.

The next spring, they began construction on a dormitory for the girls to accommodate for the number of girls attending the school. Typical of Dwight, he was hardly ever at the seminary. He trusted the people he left the seminary in the hands of and that they were dependable and talented. The students loved the seminary and their numbers increased each year.

Interpretive Comments

Northfield may not have seemed like an ideal place for many to open a seminary, but with all of Dwight Moody's travel, it was where he spent the most time. A seminary for women seems like a strange idea for the late 1870s, but with the thriving numbers of students who enrolled, obviously there was a need that the school met. Another aspect of Dwight Moody's leadership comes out in this incident with him basically leaving his vision of the seminary in the hands of those who he entrusted it to. He felt the people were very capable and he gave them complete responsibility, therefore delegating to them control over the school.

Spiritual Application

If God gives someone a vision, He expects that it will be fulfilled. God will not give a vision for ministry without blessing it. Even if the fruits of the labor are not seen to begin with, the reward for obedience will be in Heaven.

Developing Education:
Mount Hermon
Formative Encounter Ac: Upward Development
Age: 45

Incident

After Northfield Seminary opened, people in the area began to ask for a school for boys to be opened. They decided that the school should be near Northfield, but far enough away from the seminary so as to not look bad. Dwight Moody asked a friend, Hiram Camp, who was also on the seminary's board, to serve as president of the board of trustees for the boys' school. Camp also got to name the school and decided to call it Mount Hermon, coming from Psalm 133:3. The boys were of all ages and some were difficult to handle in a school atmosphere, but later boys attending the school had to be at least sixteen years old. The curriculum by 1884 made it a college preparatory school with a program in the liberal arts while still maintaining Bible and Christian doctrine classes.

Interpretive Comments

The purpose for this school and Northfield Seminary was to help young men and women who normally would have very little means to get an education receive an education that would help them further their lives for ministry. The schools existed mainly for the poor and students who had the means to pay for expensive preparatory schools were asked not to apply. Also, the schools both were well integrated with different races and both had students from foreign countries.

Spiritual Application

Training young men and women is a key in furthering the Kingdom. While increasing their knowledge in the liberal arts, one must also increase their knowledge of Biblical material and doctrine. The things that can be learned in these settings can significantly benefit the growth of the Kingdom of God.

Developing Education:
Chicago Bible Institute
Formative Encounter Ba: Ideal Role
Age: 52

Incident

Dwight Moody gradually began to sharpen his focus in the winter of 1888 deciding to go to Chicago and build a school there. Dwight expected great things to come from this idea. He felt that the hour had come to build up a class of men and women that would go to all who do not attend church and bring them into the faith. He felt this aspect of his ministry was going to succeed and he approached his idea for a school in Chicago with that confidence.

To begin with they offered seminars for training of pastors that were seen as continuing education for ministers. Then in 1889, The Bible Institute for Home and Foreign Missions was launched. With this announcement, several seminaries and pastors began to turn on Moody's idea because it was not formal education. However, to fight this thought, Moody asked R. A. Torrey to oversee the school. Torrey was a powerful preacher, teacher, and administrator. He also came with degrees from Yale and Yale Divinity School.

The purpose for the Bible institute was to recruit students who wanted to be pastor's assistants, workers in urban ministry, foreign missionaries, and English Bible teachers. They also had formalized men's and women's departments and also a music department. This Bible institute was to offer a place were practical theology could be gained unlike most seminaries where the formally trained clergy were only steeped in academic disciplines.

Interpretive Comments

Unlike the schools Dwight Moody started in Northfield, he maintained a close working relationship with this institute. He recruited students whenever he traveled and preached. He also continued to raise money for the school after it was opened to continue the development of the Bible Institute. Dwight also came up with innovations for he school, including offering evening school for working people to be able to attend. This was Dwight Moody's favorite because he saw the potential for great things to come from the training the men and women could obtain from attending classes.

Spiritual Application

Confidence in ministry is also a key. Confidence in the ministry assignment God has given you shows that you have faith that God will bless the ministry.

Finishing Well:
Publishing
Formative Encounter Aa: Upward Development
Age: 58

Incident

Dwight Moody's interest in publishing can be seen all the way back to the Civil War. However, things really began to start working in Christian publications for Dwight when he was able to convince his brother-in-law, Fleming Revell, to go into full-time Christian service publishing Christian material. There was a great need for religious material to edify Christians and help them mature in the faith. However no inexpensive materials were available for the average Christian to use and Sunday school teachers were in desperate need of materials to use. Dwight Moody recognized this need and once Revell decided to come on board with this vision, things began to get off the ground for Christian publications.

In 1869, the pair started a monthly magazine called *Everybody's Paper* and soon after their first book *Grace and Truth* by William Mackay was published. Then in 1876, Revell began to publish works by Dwight himself. These were printed in pamphlet form and were followed by hardbound volumes of sermons. From 1880 until 1899 with Dwight's death, Revell's company was basically maintained with printing Moody's works. Dwight Moody was not the only author Revell's company printed material by. Dwight also recruited major Christian figures to have their works published and soon there after works were published about answered prayer, divine healing, etc.

Dwight promoted the sale of these books whenever he preached and he used the money earned from them to buy books to give away or for scholarships for students at his schools. In the early 1890s, Christian books became very scarce. For one reason, the books were very expensive and also most bookstores did not carry Christian material. Dwight Moody got an idea to take after the successful dime novels and vault Christian works in the same fashion making them cheap and easy to find. He felt a sense of urgency about his plan and finally he got Revell on board. They designed their Christian literature to combine five features: popular style, well-known authors, non-denominational content, low price, and high quality workmanship.

Interpretive Comments

Again, Dwight Moody saw a need and had a vision of a plan to attempt to resolve the problem. Moody's desire to see souls saved was the driving force and this ministry could be performed after he was gone. He was also interested in seeing converts nurtured through this work.

Spiritual Application

Once your ministry is developed, not only do you have the responsibility of winning souls for Christ but also you have to be responsible for maturing the disciples, nurturing the converts, and helping them reproduce your ministry or finding their own.

Finishing Well:
Christian Conferences
Formative Encounter Ba: Ideal Role
Age: 50s

Incident

Dwight Moody had seen Christian conferences in England and there were many in the United States, but after prayer he realized that what he was called to do had to be something new. In 1880, Dwight Moody held his first Northfield Conference for ten days. This conference led to many others that were very influential to the lives of those who came. Workers from every state and also furlough missionaries would come to the conferences that were mostly devoted to prayer. Moody would often talk about how the church lacked power to change people's lives because it leaned too much on things besides prayer, the Holy Spirit, and the Bible. Dwight saw these conferences as times of first-rate education and spiritual refreshment.

These conferences at Northfield were not just for pastors and people in ministry, but Moody also developed college student conferences. He planned for them to be mainly for YMCA workers who had a calling to work with college outreaches. The conferences were called "College Students' Summer School" and were prized for their ethnic and international diversity. They would often have sons of missionaries along with young men from all over the world. With the college students, Dwight basically let them arrange the conference themselves but maintaining the core Bible study and prayer sessions. What the young men prized most of all was the question and answer sessions they had with Dwight Moody and other leading figures of Christianity.

Interpretive Comments

Northfield, Massachusetts became an important year-round training center for Christian ministry. Christians from all over the world and from all ages, came to find formal and informal Christian education to equip them for whatever God's call was for their lives. Several thousand men and women would come through the conferences every year and then would head out with their knowledge and vision to change the world.

Spiritual Application

The richness of the Holy Spirit blessing a ministry can be seen in many places. Dwight Moody sets a wonderful example of prayer in ministry. Instead of seeing a need, moving into the ministry, and then asking the Lord to bless it Dwight would first ask the Lord for direction to a ripe harvest and then move into the ministry God directed him to.

Discovery Statement

In conclusion, this study has been a significant help to me personally. Looking through D. L. Moody's life and seeing how the Lord used him for various ministries was amazing. The most important thing that stuck out to me was that instead of moving into a ministry and then praying for a blessing from the Lord, D. L. Moody would wait and pray for direction to find which ministry field to go to. Prayer for direction from the Lord instead of expecting the Lord to follow us into ministry was a significant fact I will take away from this.

My expectations for this study were all met and exceeded. I was able to see D. L. Moody take the people he came into contact with and use them to better the Kingdom in whatever way he needed. If he needed a speaker, he would find a speaker from among the least likely people. If he needed money for a ministry project, he had no trouble finding support in the short amount of time. It was amazing to see how the Lord blessed the ministries he touched and therefore also the people around him.

D. L. Moody's spiritual life was in a league of its own. He seemed to always be growing toward something better instead of remaining stagnate. His continual growth made this study very interesting because he would learn something and then continue to seek more knowledge. Instead of seeking knowledge from books, Moody often preferred practical theology and ministry assignments to learn from.

There were many leadership applications that were seen in his ministry. Sometimes he did not implement leadership theories correctly, but he had mastered the idea of delegating in the later years of his ministry. One of his key ministries was developing other leaders. He always believed there were greater things to come after him and he wanted to have a part in developing those leaders.

Overall, this study has been very helpful to me in helping me to see the leadership theories discussed in class put into a practical ministry situation. Not only in leadership has it helped me, but also studying his life has shaped me spiritually. Some of the keys of knowledge he learned from others on how to study the Bible are wonderful ways to get more out of what you are reading. I am looking forward to putting some of what I learned spiritually into practice personally.

Bibliography

Clinton, J. Robert. *The Making of a Leader*. Colorado Springs: Navpress, 1973.

Dorsett, Lyle. *The Life of D. L. Moody: A Passion for Souls*. Chicago: Moody Press, 1986.

About the Authors:

Richard L. Gray, Ph. D.,
Professor: Leadership and Christian Ministries
Asbury Seminary

After completing degrees at the Th. M. and Ph. D. levels in Christian Leadership and serving as National Director for Ethnic Leadership Development for both the Lausanne Committee for World Evangelization and World Vision US Ministries, Dr. Gray came to Asbury Seminary in the fall of 1999 and helped establish the institutions Master of Arts in Christian Leadership which he now oversees as department head. In addition to his service at Asbury Seminary, Dr. Gray serves as Executive Director of The Obsidian Society. He and his wife (Coral) make their home on the outskirts of Lexington, Kentucky.

Coral A. Gray
Adjunct Professor: Leadership Department
Asbury Seminary

After completing a Master of Theology at Fuller Seminary, Mrs. Gray entered the PhD program in Intercultural Studies at Asbury Seminary where she serves the Christian Leadership department as adjunct faculty. Additionally, she serves on the National Board of Directors for both Ichthus Ministries and The Obsidian Society.